DIBELS® Next Progress Monitoring Assessment Book A: Assessor Directions and Student Materials

Roland H. Good III

Ruth A. Kaminski

with: Kelli Cummings, Chantal Dufour-Martel, Kathleen Petersen,
Kelly Powell-Smith, Stephanie Stollar, and Joshua Wallin

Dynamic Measurement Group, Inc.

DIBELS is a registered trademark of Dynamic Measurement Group, Inc. Visit our Web site at www.dibels.org.

(Revised: 04/06/10)

ISBN 13: 978-1-60697-388-2
ISBN 10: 1-60697-388-6

273201/354/03-12

Printed in the United States of America

Published and Distributed by

4093 Specialty Place • Longmont, Colorado 80504
(303) 651-2829 • www.soprislearning.com

How to Use This Book

This book includes the necessary student materials and the directions for administering each measure to students. Before administering the progress monitoring assessment, be sure you have read the *DIBELS Next Assessment Manual* and have practiced administering these measures so that you are comfortable using them with students.

You will also need one copy of the appropriate Progress Monitoring Scoring Booklet for each student, to record the student's responses and scores.

First Sound Fluency and Phoneme Segmentation Fluency do not include student materials. For these measures, read the instructions from this book and read the test items from the scoring booklet.

During testing, this book should lay flat on a desk or table, with the student materials placed directly in front of the student. The assessor directions and instructions to read to the student are located on the opposite page for ease of use. Be sure to remove any other possible distractions from the testing surface.

Please refer to the *DIBELS Next Assessment Manual* for more information on administering and scoring each *DIBELS Next* measure.

FSF

PSF

NWF

Table of Contents

FSF

PSF

NWF

Directions: Make sure you have reviewed the scoring rules in the *DIBELS Next Assessment Manual* and have them available. Say these specific directions to the student:

▶ **Practice item #1)** *Listen to me say this word, "man." The first sound that you hear in the word "man" is /mmm/. Listen. /mmm/. "Man." What is the first sound you hear in the word "man"?*

Correct response /mmm/ or /ma/	**Good. /mmm/ is the first sound in "man."**					(Present practice item #2.)
Incorrect response Student does not respond within 3 <u>seconds</u> or responds <u>incorrectly</u>	**/mmm/ is the first sound you hear in the word "man." Listen. /mmm/. "Man." Say it with me. /mmm/. Let's try it again. What is the first sound you hear in the word "man"?**	Correct response	**Good.**			(Present practice item #2.)
		Incorrect response	**/mmm/. Say /mmm/.**	Correct	**Good.**	(Present practice item #2.)
				Incorrect	**Okay.**	(Present practice item #2.)

▶ **Practice item #2)** *Listen to me say another word, "moon." What is the first sound you hear in the word "moon"?*

Correct response /mmm/ or /moo/	**Good. /mmm/ is the first sound in "moon."**					(Present practice item #3.)
Incorrect response Student does not respond within 3 <u>seconds</u> or responds <u>incorrectly</u>	**/mmm/ is the first sound you hear in the word "moon." Listen. /mmm/. "Moon." Say it with me. /mmm/. Let's try it again. What is the first sound you hear in the word "moon"?**	Correct response	**Good.**			(Present practice item #3.)
		Incorrect response	**/mmm/. Say /mmm/.**	Correct	**Good.**	(Present practice item #3.)
				Incorrect	**Okay.**	(Present practice item #3.)

▶ **Go to the next page.**

▶ **Practice item #3)** *Let's try another word, "sun."* (Wait up to 3 seconds for student to respond.) If the student does not respond, ask, *What is the first sound you hear in the word "sun"?*

Correct response /sss/ or /su/	**Good. /sss/ is the first sound in "sun."**		(Begin testing.)			
Incorrect response Student does not respond within 3 <u>seconds</u> or responds <u>incorrectly</u>	**/sss/ is the first sound you hear in the word "sun." Listen. /sss/. "Sun." Say it with me. /sss/. Let's try it again. What is the first sound you hear in the word "sun"?**	Correct response	**Good.**	(Begin testing.)		
		Incorrect response	**/sss/. Say /sss/.**	Correct	**Good.**	(Begin testing.)
				Incorrect	**Okay.**	(Begin testing.)

▶ **Begin testing.** *Now I am going to say more words. You tell me the first sound you hear in the word.* (Say the first word from the list in the scoring booklet.)

Timing	1 minute. Start your stopwatch after saying the first test item.
Wait	If the student does not respond within 3 seconds on a word, mark a slash (**/**) through the zero and say the next word.
Discontinue	If no sounds are correct in the first five words, discontinue and record a score of 0.
Reminders	If you think the student may have forgotten the task, say ***Remember to tell me the <u>first</u> sound that you hear in the word.*** Immediately say the next word. (Repeat as often as needed.)

If the student says the name of the letter, say ***Remember to tell me the first <u>sound</u> in the word, not the letter name.*** Immediately say the next word. (Allowed one time.) |

FSF

Directions: Make sure you have reviewed the scoring rules in the *DIBELS Next Assessment Manual* and have them available. Say these specific directions to the student:

▶ *We are going to say the sounds in words. Listen to me say all the sounds in the word "fan." /f/ /a/ /n/. Listen to another word,* (pause) *"jump." /j/ /u/ /m/ /p/. Your turn. Say all the sounds in "soap."*

Correct response /s/ /oa/ /p/	**Very good saying all the sounds in "soap."**	(Begin testing.)

Incorrect response anything other than /s/ /oa/ /p/	**I said "soap," so you say /s/ /oa/ /p/. Your turn. Say all the sounds in "soap."**	*Correct response*	**Very good.**	(Begin testing.)
		Incorrect response	**Okay.**	(Begin testing.)

▶ **Begin testing.** *I am going to say more words. I will say the word, and you say all the sounds in the word.* (Say the first word from the list in the scoring booklet.)

Timing	1 minute. Start your stopwatch after saying the first test item.
Wait	If the student does not respond within 3 seconds, say the next word.
Discontinue	If no sound segments are correct in the first five words, discontinue and record a score of 0.
Reminders	If the student spells the word, say **Say the <u>sounds</u> in the word.** Immediately say the next word. (Allowed one time.)
	If the student repeats the word, say **Remember to say all the sounds in the word.** Immediately say the next word. (Allowed one time.)

PSF

sog   mip

1 DIBELS® Nonsense Word Fluency
Progress Monitoring 1

Directions: Make sure you have reviewed the scoring rules in the *DIBELS Next Assessment Manual* and have them available. Say these specific directions to the student:

▶ *We are going to read some make-believe words. Listen. This word is "sog."* (Run your finger under the word as you say it.) *The sounds are /s/ /o/ /g/* (point to each letter). *Your turn. Read this make-believe word* (point to the word "mip"). *If you can't read the whole word, tell me any sounds you know.*

Correct Whole Word Read mip	***Very good reading the word "mip."***	(Begin testing.)

Correct Letter Sounds Any other response with all the correct letter sounds	***Very good.*** /m/ /i/ /p/ (point to each letter) ***or "mip"*** (run your finger under the word as you say it).	(Begin testing.)

Incorrect response No response within 3 <u>seconds</u>, or response includes any errors	***Listen.*** /m/ /i/ /p/ ***or "mip."*** (Run your finger under the letters as you say the sounds.) ***Your turn. Read this make-believe word.*** (Point to the word "mip.") ***If you can't read the whole word, tell me any sounds you know.***	*Correct response*	***Very good.***	(Begin testing.)
		Incorrect response	***Okay.***	(Begin testing.)

▶ Begin testing. *I would like you to read more make-believe words. Do your best reading. If you can't read the whole word, tell me any sounds you know.* Go to the next page.

▶ hif	mez	un	jaf	roc
liv	rem	vam	ov	luf
yej	lig	zat	hof	puj
ib	maj	wos	keb	ruk
ug	jin	pag	bom	sez
des	woj	lut	rav	zil
kun	aj	yim	rev	kol
huf	soz	zas	dif	em
ked	tov	zuv	paf	jip
vap	id	muj	sec	sol

1 DIBELS® Nonsense Word Fluency
Progress Monitoring 1 continued

▶ *Put your finger under the first word. Ready, begin.*

Timing	1 minute. Start your stopwatch after telling the student to begin. Place a bracket (**]**) and say **Stop** after 1 minute.
Wait	If the student responds sound-by-sound, mixes sounds and words, or sounds out and recodes, allow 3 seconds, then provide the correct letter sound.
	If the student responds with whole words, allow 3 seconds, then provide the correct word.
Discontinue	If the student has no correct letter sounds in the first line, say **Stop** and record a score of 0.
Reminders	If the student does not read from left to right, say **Go this way**. (Sweep your finger across the row.) (Allowed one time.)
	If the student says letter names, say **Say the sounds, not the letter names**. (Allowed one time.)
	If the student reads the word first, then says the letter sounds, say **Just read the word**. (Allowed one time.)
	If the student says all of the letter sounds correctly in the first row, but does not make any attempt to blend or recode, say **Try to read the words as whole words**.
	If the student stops (and it's not a hesitation on a specific item), say **Keep going**. (Repeat as often as needed.)
	If the student loses his/her place, point. (Repeat as often as needed.)

NWF

sog   mip

2 DIBELS® Nonsense Word Fluency
Progress Monitoring 2

Directions: Make sure you have reviewed the scoring rules in the *DIBELS Next Assessment Manual* and have them available. Say these specific directions to the student:

▶ *We are going to read some make-believe words. Listen. This word is "sog."* (Run your finger under the word as you say it.) *The sounds are /s/ /o/ /g/* (point to each letter). *Your turn. Read this make-believe word* (point to the word "mip"). *If you can't read the whole word, tell me any sounds you know.*

Correct Whole Word Read mip	***Very good reading the word "mip."***	(Begin testing.)		
Correct Letter Sounds Any other response with all the correct letter sounds	***Very good. /m/ /i/ /p/*** (point to each letter) ***or "mip"*** (run your finger under the word as you say it).	(Begin testing.)		
Incorrect response No response within 3 <u>seconds</u>, or response includes any errors	***Listen. /m/ /i/ /p/ or "mip."*** (Run your finger under the letters as you say the sounds.) ***Your turn. Read this make-believe word.*** (Point to the word "mip.") ***If you can't read the whole word, tell me any sounds you know.***	Correct response	***Very good.***	(Begin testing.)
		Incorrect response	***Okay.***	(Begin testing.)

▶ **Begin testing.** *I would like you to read more make-believe words. Do your best reading. If you can't read the whole word, tell me any sounds you know.* Go to the next page.

▶ ris	baj	uk	zom	het
foj	muc	yeb	iv	baf
yaz	mol	zet	pid	luv
im	loz	jeg	kal	fub
ot	juf	fal	neb	diz
huc	wiv	mes	pav	zol
dus	oj	jes	tiz	mak
rud	sej	wac	mis	os
bis	bez	jav	tuf	joc
zin	ub	tej	bal	lof

2 DIBELS® Nonsense Word Fluency
Progress Monitoring 2 continued

▶ *Put your finger under the first word. Ready, begin.*

Timing	1 minute. Start your stopwatch after telling the student to begin. Place a bracket ( ]) and say **Stop** after 1 minute.
Wait	If the student responds sound-by-sound, mixes sounds and words, or sounds out and recodes, allow 3 seconds, then provide the correct letter sound.
	If the student responds with whole words, allow 3 seconds, then provide the correct word.
Discontinue	If the student has no correct letter sounds in the first line, say **Stop** and record a score of 0.
Reminders	If the student does not read from left to right, say **Go this way**. (Sweep your finger across the row.) (Allowed one time.)
	If the student says letter names, say **Say the sounds, not the letter names**. (Allowed one time.)
	If the student reads the word first, then says the letter sounds, say **Just read the word**. (Allowed one time.)
	If the student says all of the letter sounds correctly in the first row, but does not make any attempt to blend or recode, say **Try to read the words as whole words**.
	If the student stops (and it's not a hesitation on a specific item), say **Keep going**. (Repeat as often as needed.)
	If the student loses his/her place, point. (Repeat as often as needed.)

NWF

sog   mip

3 DIBELS® Nonsense Word Fluency
Progress Monitoring 3

Directions: Make sure you have reviewed the scoring rules in the *DIBELS Next Assessment Manual* and have them available. Say these specific directions to the student:

► ***We are going to read some make-believe words. Listen. This word is "sog."*** (Run your finger under the word as you say it.) ***The sounds are /s/ /o/ /g/*** (point to each letter). ***Your turn. Read this make-believe word*** (point to the word "mip"). ***If you can't read the whole word, tell me any sounds you know.***

Correct Whole Word Read mip	***Very good reading the word "mip."***	(Begin testing.)
Correct Letter Sounds Any other response with all the correct letter sounds	***Very good. /m/ /i/ /p/*** (point to each letter) ***or "mip"*** (run your finger under the word as you say it)***.***	(Begin testing.)

Incorrect response No response within 3 <u>seconds</u>, or response includes any errors	***Listen. /m/ /i/ /p/ or "mip."*** (Run your finger under the letters as you say the sounds.) ***Your turn. Read this make-believe word.*** (Point to the word "mip.") ***If you can't read the whole word, tell me any sounds you know.***	*Correct response*	***Very good.***	(Begin testing.)
		Incorrect response	***Okay.***	(Begin testing.)

► **Begin testing.** ***I would like you to read more make-believe words. Do your best reading. If you can't read the whole word, tell me any sounds you know.*** **Go to the next page.**

► sek	tav	og	yuk	lil
mav	nef	vif	uz	non
jez	fid	yud	mot	sav
ep	poz	zal	suf	bil
od	vil	teb	nuc	nav
dep	zoj	ras	luz	wic
bof	ev	zun	fav	mim
dom	tiv	zes	haf	un
lol	nij	jaj	puc	zem
yef	um	miv	pof	pac

3 DIBELS® Nonsense Word Fluency
Progress Monitoring 3 continued

► *Put your finger under the first word. Ready, begin.*

Timing	1 minute. Start your stopwatch after telling the student to begin. Place a bracket (**]**) and say **Stop** after 1 minute.
Wait	If the student responds sound-by-sound, mixes sounds and words, or sounds out and recodes, allow 3 seconds, then provide the correct letter sound.
	If the student responds with whole words, allow 3 seconds, then provide the correct word.
Discontinue	If the student has no correct letter sounds in the first line, say **Stop** and record a score of 0.
Reminders	If the student does not read from left to right, say **Go this way**. (Sweep your finger across the row.) (Allowed one time.)
	If the student says letter names, say **Say the sounds, not the letter names**. (Allowed one time.)
	If the student reads the word first, then says the letter sounds, say **Just read the word**. (Allowed one time.)
	If the student says all of the letter sounds correctly in the first row, but does not make any attempt to blend or recode, say **Try to read the words as whole words**.
	If the student stops (and it's not a hesitation on a specific item), say **Keep going**. (Repeat as often as needed.)
	If the student loses his/her place, point. (Repeat as often as needed.)

NWF

sog   mip

4 DIBELS® Nonsense Word Fluency
Progress Monitoring 4

Directions: Make sure you have reviewed the scoring rules in the *DIBELS Next Assessment Manual* and have them available. Say these specific directions to the student:

▶ ***We are going to read some make-believe words. Listen. This word is "sog."*** (Run your finger under the word as you say it.) ***The sounds are /s/ /o/ /g/*** (point to each letter). ***Your turn. Read this make-believe word*** (point to the word "mip"). ***If you can't read the whole word, tell me any sounds you know.***

Correct Whole Word Read mip	***Very good reading the word "mip."***	(Begin testing.)
Correct Letter Sounds Any other response with all the correct letter sounds	***Very good. /m/ /i/ /p/*** (point to each letter) ***or "mip"*** (run your finger under the word as you say it)***.***	(Begin testing.)

Incorrect response No response within 3 <u>seconds</u>, or response includes any errors	***Listen. /m/ /i/ /p/ or "mip."*** (Run your finger under the letters as you say the sounds.) ***Your turn. Read this make-believe word.*** (Point to the word "mip.") ***If you can't read the whole word, tell me any sounds you know.***	*Correct response*	***Very good.***	(Begin testing.)
		Incorrect response	***Okay.***	(Begin testing.)

▶ ***Begin testing.*** *I would like you to read more make-believe words. Do your best reading. If you can't read the whole word, tell me any sounds you know.* **Go to the next page.**

► lun	naj	ec	zob	tig
bov	fim	vac	uj	hed
wov	dek	vun	hac	riv
af	huz	vim	seg	nop
oc	zeb	kam	tul	hiz
nad	zez	rop	ruj	wis
lak	ij	wun	boz	kec
pib	bav	wuc	bol	ek
meb	maj	juv	dit	zok
yec	ob	niz	buc	rak

4 DIBELS® Nonsense Word Fluency
Progress Monitoring 4 continued

▶ *Put your finger under the first word. Ready, begin.*

Timing	1 minute. Start your stopwatch after telling the student to begin. Place a bracket ( ]) and say **Stop** after 1 minute.
Wait	If the student responds sound-by-sound, mixes sounds and words, or sounds out and recodes, allow 3 seconds, then provide the correct letter sound.
	If the student responds with whole words, allow 3 seconds, then provide the correct word.
Discontinue	If the student has no correct letter sounds in the first line, say **Stop** and record a score of 0.
Reminders	If the student does not read from left to right, say **Go this way**. (Sweep your finger across the row.) (Allowed one time.)
	If the student says letter names, say **Say the sounds, not the letter names**. (Allowed one time.)
	If the student reads the word first, then says the letter sounds, say **Just read the word**. (Allowed one time.)
	If the student says all of the letter sounds correctly in the first row, but does not make any attempt to blend or recode, say **Try to read the words as whole words**.
	If the student stops (and it's not a hesitation on a specific item), say **Keep going**. (Repeat as often as needed.)
	If the student loses his/her place, point. (Repeat as often as needed.)

NWF

sog   mip

5 DIBELS® Nonsense Word Fluency
Progress Monitoring 5

Directions: Make sure you have reviewed the scoring rules in the *DIBELS Next Assessment Manual* and have them available. Say these specific directions to the student:

▶ *We are going to read some make-believe words. Listen. This word is "sog."* (Run your finger under the word as you say it.) *The sounds are /s/ /o/ /g/* (point to each letter). *Your turn. Read this make-believe word* (point to the word "mip"). *If you can't read the whole word, tell me any sounds you know.*

Correct Whole Word Read mip	*Very good reading the word "mip."*	(Begin testing.)
Correct Letter Sounds Any other response with all the correct letter sounds	*Very good. /m/ /i/ /p/* (point to each letter) *or "mip"* (run your finger under the word as you say it).	(Begin testing.)

Incorrect response No response within 3 <u>seconds</u>, or response includes any errors	*Listen. /m/ /i/ /p/ or "mip."* (Run your finger under the letters as you say the sounds.) *Your turn. Read this make-believe word.* (Point to the word "mip.") *If you can't read the whole word, tell me any sounds you know.*	*Correct response*	**Very good.**	(Begin testing.)
		Incorrect response	**Okay.**	(Begin testing.)

▶ **Begin testing.** *I would like you to read more make-believe words. Do your best reading. If you can't read the whole word, tell me any sounds you know.* **Go to the next page.**

▶ lim	saj	ug	yot	fep
dej	tas	yop	ij	dun
zov	sal	yit	ped	muv
ic	kav	veg	dop	kuk
ul	waf	pok	mel	biv
ret	vuv	hin	roj	jad
fen	av	zot	biz	lud
sug	dij	yat	nog	el
mef	piz	zav	pul	zof
wob	em	hij	kas	kuc

▶ *Put your finger under the first word. Ready, begin.*

Timing	1 minute. Start your stopwatch after telling the student to begin. Place a bracket (**]**) and say **Stop** after 1 minute.
Wait	If the student responds sound-by-sound, mixes sounds and words, or sounds out and recodes, allow 3 seconds, then provide the correct letter sound. If the student responds with whole words, allow 3 seconds, then provide the correct word.
Discontinue	If the student has no correct letter sounds in the first line, say **Stop** and record a score of 0.
Reminders	If the student does not read from left to right, say **Go this way**. (Sweep your finger across the row.) (Allowed one time.) If the student says letter names, say **Say the sounds, not the letter names**. (Allowed one time.) If the student reads the word first, then says the letter sounds, say **Just read the word**. (Allowed one time.) If the student says all of the letter sounds correctly in the first row, but does not make any attempt to blend or recode, say **Try to read the words as whole words**. If the student stops (and it's not a hesitation on a specific item), say **Keep going**. (Repeat as often as needed.) If the student loses his/her place, point. (Repeat as often as needed.)

NWF

sog   mip

6 DIBELS® Nonsense Word Fluency
Progress Monitoring 6

Directions: Make sure you have reviewed the scoring rules in the *DIBELS Next Assessment Manual* and have them available. Say these specific directions to the student:

▶ *We are going to read some make-believe words. Listen. This word is "sog."* (Run your finger under the word as you say it.) *The sounds are /s/ /o/ /g/* (point to each letter). *Your turn. Read this make-believe word* (point to the word "mip"). *If you can't read the whole word, tell me any sounds you know.*

Correct Whole Word Read mip	*Very good reading the word "mip."*	(Begin testing.)
Correct Letter Sounds Any other response with all the correct letter sounds	*Very good. /m/ /i/ /p/* (point to each letter) *or "mip"* (run your finger under the word as you say it).	(Begin testing.)

Incorrect response No response within 3 <u>seconds</u>, or response includes any errors	*Listen. /m/ /i/ /p/ or "mip."* (Run your finger under the letters as you say the sounds.) *Your turn. Read this make-believe word.* (Point to the word "mip.") *If you can't read the whole word, tell me any sounds you know.*	*Correct response*	**Very good.**	(Begin testing.)
		Incorrect response	**Okay.**	(Begin testing.)

▶ **Begin testing.** *I would like you to read more make-believe words. Do your best reading. If you can't read the whole word, tell me any sounds you know.* Go to the next page.

▶ hos	bev	ab	zut	mig
pav	loc	yeg	uj	tid
jev	sif	jop	tac	tuz
ib	mev	jus	bac	kon
ud	vaf	kel	fod	riz
ses	yuj	mon	rij	vad
dat	iv	zuf	lov	neg
bas	miz	jom	mep	uc
rik	fez	zuj	pon	wam
zon	id	fej	maf	duk

6 DIBELS® Nonsense Word Fluency
Progress Monitoring 6 continued

▶ *Put your finger under the first word. Ready, begin.*

Timing	1 minute. Start your stopwatch after telling the student to begin. Place a bracket ( ]) and say **Stop** after 1 minute.
Wait	If the student responds sound-by-sound, mixes sounds and words, or sounds out and recodes, allow 3 seconds, then provide the correct letter sound.
	If the student responds with whole words, allow 3 seconds, then provide the correct word.
Discontinue	If the student has no correct letter sounds in the first line, say **Stop** and record a score of 0.
Reminders	If the student does not read from left to right, say **Go this way**. (Sweep your finger across the row.) (Allowed one time.)
	If the student says letter names, say **Say the sounds, not the letter names**. (Allowed one time.)
	If the student reads the word first, then says the letter sounds, say **Just read the word**. (Allowed one time.)
	If the student says all of the letter sounds correctly in the first row, but does not make any attempt to blend or recode, say **Try to read the words as whole words**.
	If the student stops (and it's not a hesitation on a specific item), say **Keep going**. (Repeat as often as needed.)
	If the student loses his/her place, point. (Repeat as often as needed.)

NWF

sog   mip

7 DIBELS® Nonsense Word Fluency
Progress Monitoring 7

Directions: Make sure you have reviewed the scoring rules in the *DIBELS Next Assessment Manual* and have them available. Say these specific directions to the student:

▶ *We are going to read some make-believe words. Listen. This word is "sog."* (Run your finger under the word as you say it.) *The sounds are /s/ /o/ /g/* (point to each letter). *Your turn. Read this make-believe word* (point to the word "mip"). *If you can't read the whole word, tell me any sounds you know.*

Correct Whole Word Read mip	***Very good reading the word "mip."***	(Begin testing.)
Correct Letter Sounds Any other response with all the correct letter sounds	***Very good. /m/ /i/ /p/*** (point to each letter) ***or "mip"*** (run your finger under the word as you say it).	(Begin testing.)

Incorrect response No response within 3 <u>seconds</u>, or response includes any errors	***Listen. /m/ /i/ /p/ or "mip."*** (Run your finger under the letters as you say the sounds.) ***Your turn. Read this make-believe word.*** (Point to the word "mip.") ***If you can't read the whole word, tell me any sounds you know.***	*Correct response*	***Very good.***	(Begin testing.)
		Incorrect response	***Okay.***	(Begin testing.)

▶ **Begin testing.** *I would like you to read more make-believe words. Do your best reading. If you can't read the whole word, tell me any sounds you know.* **Go to the next page.**

► nim	duz	ak	zek	dok
rav	lin	vod	ev	nus
vez	kac	yib	duc	hoj
op	tij	jak	det	nup
ef	yof	pik	nub	laj
sok	yij	def	raj	vus
faf	oj	weg	niv	lum
fom	kij	wal	mec	ut
lef	mij	vuj	mog	vas
vib	ap	ruz	reg	mof

7 DIBELS® Nonsense Word Fluency
Progress Monitoring 7 continued

▶ *Put your finger under the first word. Ready, begin.*

Timing	1 minute. Start your stopwatch after telling the student to begin. Place a bracket (**]**) and say *Stop* after 1 minute.
Wait	If the student responds sound-by-sound, mixes sounds and words, or sounds out and recodes, allow 3 seconds, then provide the correct letter sound. If the student responds with whole words, allow 3 seconds, then provide the correct word.
Discontinue	If the student has no correct letter sounds in the first line, say *Stop* and record a score of 0.
Reminders	If the student does not read from left to right, say *Go this way*. (Sweep your finger across the row.) (Allowed one time.) If the student says letter names, say *Say the sounds, not the letter names*. (Allowed one time.) If the student reads the word first, then says the letter sounds, say *Just read the word*. (Allowed one time.) If the student says all of the letter sounds correctly in the first row, but does not make any attempt to blend or recode, say *Try to read the words as whole words*. If the student stops (and it's not a hesitation on a specific item), say *Keep going*. (Repeat as often as needed.) If the student loses his/her place, point. (Repeat as often as needed.)

sog   mip

8 DIBELS® Nonsense Word Fluency
Progress Monitoring 8

Directions: Make sure you have reviewed the scoring rules in the *DIBELS Next Assessment Manual* and have them available. Say these specific directions to the student:

► *We are going to read some make-believe words. Listen. This word is "sog."* (Run your finger under the word as you say it.) *The sounds are /s/ /o/ /g/* (point to each letter). *Your turn. Read this make-believe word* (point to the word "mip"). *If you can't read the whole word, tell me any sounds you know.*

Correct Whole Word Read mip	**Very good reading the word "mip."**	(Begin testing.)
Correct Letter Sounds Any other response with all the correct letter sounds	**Very good.** */m/ /i/ /p/* (point to each letter) **or "mip"** (run your finger under the word as you say it).	(Begin testing.)

Incorrect response No response within 3 <u>seconds</u>, or response includes any errors	**Listen.** */m/ /i/ /p/* **or "mip."** (Run your finger under the letters as you say the sounds.) **Your turn. Read this make-believe word.** (Point to the word "mip.") **If you can't read the whole word, tell me any sounds you know.**	*Correct response*	**Very good.**	(Begin testing.)
		Incorrect response	**Okay.**	(Begin testing.)

► **Begin testing.** *I would like you to read more make-believe words. Do your best reading. If you can't read the whole word, tell me any sounds you know.* **Go to the next page.**

▶ nam	muz	et	wom	fip
doj	las	zef	uv	fis
zoz	tem	vid	lub	faj
ag	doz	vis	tuc	pec
uf	wik	tet	mod	dav
dec	viv	rom	daj	yuf
fob	az	zib	fev	ruf
hes	koj	wus	kig	ac
hal	luj	ziv	kod	wem
vut	eb	paj	hib	noc

8 DIBELS® Nonsense Word Fluency
Progress Monitoring 8 continued

▶ *Put your finger under the first word. Ready, begin.*

Timing	1 minute. Start your stopwatch after telling the student to begin. Place a bracket ( ]) and say *Stop* after 1 minute.
Wait	If the student responds sound-by-sound, mixes sounds and words, or sounds out and recodes, allow 3 seconds, then provide the correct letter sound.
	If the student responds with whole words, allow 3 seconds, then provide the correct word.
Discontinue	If the student has no correct letter sounds in the first line, say *Stop* and record a score of 0.
Reminders	If the student does not read from left to right, say *Go this way*. (Sweep your finger across the row.) (Allowed one time.)
	If the student says letter names, say *Say the sounds, not the letter names*. (Allowed one time.)
	If the student reads the word first, then says the letter sounds, say *Just read the word*. (Allowed one time.)
	If the student says all of the letter sounds correctly in the first row, but does not make any attempt to blend or recode, say *Try to read the words as whole words*.
	If the student stops (and it's not a hesitation on a specific item), say *Keep going*. (Repeat as often as needed.)
	If the student loses his/her place, point. (Repeat as often as needed.)

NWF

sog   mip

9 DIBELS® Nonsense Word Fluency
Progress Monitoring 9

Directions: Make sure you have reviewed the scoring rules in the *DIBELS Next Assessment Manual* and have them available. Say these specific directions to the student:

▶ *We are going to read some make-believe words. Listen. This word is "sog."* (Run your finger under the word as you say it.) *The sounds are /s/ /o/ /g/* (point to each letter). *Your turn. Read this make-believe word* (point to the word "mip"). *If you can't read the whole word, tell me any sounds you know.*

Correct Whole Word Read mip	*Very good reading the word "mip."*	(Begin testing.)
Correct Letter Sounds Any other response with all the correct letter sounds	*Very good. /m/ /i/ /p/* (point to each letter) *or "mip"* (run your finger under the word as you say it).	(Begin testing.)

Incorrect response No response within 3 <u>seconds</u>, or response includes any errors	*Listen. /m/ /i/ /p/ or "mip."* (Run your finger under the letters as you say the sounds.) *Your turn. Read this make-believe word.* (Point to the word "mip.") *If you can't read the whole word, tell me any sounds you know.*	*Correct response*	*Very good.*	(Begin testing.)
		Incorrect response	*Okay.*	(Begin testing.)

▶ **Begin testing.** *I would like you to read more make-believe words. Do your best reading. If you can't read the whole word, tell me any sounds you know.* Go to the next page.

▶ sid	buj	eg	vok	hab
soj	feg	zac	uz	mid
juz	hak	wif	nem	moz
ig	koz	jum	nep	kat
om	zel	sac	fik	nuz
laf	wej	kip	puv	von
sas	ov	yic	sev	tum
bes	kaj	yug	hil	ol
sup	mov	yav	sep	vig
jol	en	puz	lac	mil

9 DIBELS® Nonsense Word Fluency
Progress Monitoring 9 continued

▶ *Put your finger under the first word. Ready, begin.*

Timing	1 minute. Start your stopwatch after telling the student to begin. Place a bracket ( ]) and say **Stop** after 1 minute.
Wait	If the student responds sound-by-sound, mixes sounds and words, or sounds out and recodes, allow 3 seconds, then provide the correct letter sound. If the student responds with whole words, allow 3 seconds, then provide the correct word.
Discontinue	If the student has no correct letter sounds in the first line, say **Stop** and record a score of 0.
Reminders	If the student does not read from left to right, say **Go this way**. (Sweep your finger across the row.) (Allowed one time.) If the student says letter names, say **Say the sounds, not the letter names**. (Allowed one time.) If the student reads the word first, then says the letter sounds, say **Just read the word**. (Allowed one time.) If the student says all of the letter sounds correctly in the first row, but does not make any attempt to blend or recode, say **Try to read the words as whole words**. If the student stops (and it's not a hesitation on a specific item), say **Keep going**. (Repeat as often as needed.) If the student loses his/her place, point. (Repeat as often as needed.)

NWF

sog   mip

10 DIBELS® Nonsense Word Fluency
Progress Monitoring 10

Directions: Make sure you have reviewed the scoring rules in the *DIBELS Next Assessment Manual* and have them available. Say these specific directions to the student:

▶ *We are going to read some make-believe words. Listen. This word is "sog."* (Run your finger under the word as you say it.) *The sounds are /s/ /o/ /g/* (point to each letter). *Your turn. Read this make-believe word* (point to the word "mip"). *If you can't read the whole word, tell me any sounds you know.*

Correct Whole Word Read mip	**Very good reading the word "mip."**	(Begin testing.)
Correct Letter Sounds Any other response with all the correct letter sounds	**Very good. /m/ /i/ /p/** (point to each letter) **or "mip"** (run your finger under the word as you say it).	(Begin testing.)

Incorrect response No response within 3 <u>seconds</u>, or response includes any errors	**Listen. /m/ /i/ /p/ or "mip."** (Run your finger under the letters as you say the sounds.) **Your turn. Read this make-believe word.** (Point to the word "mip.") **If you can't read the whole word, tell me any sounds you know.**	*Correct response*	**Very good.**	(Begin testing.)
		Incorrect response	**Okay.**	(Begin testing.)

▶ **Begin testing.** *I would like you to read more make-believe words. Do your best reading. If you can't read the whole word, tell me any sounds you know.* **Go to the next page.**

► sen	nuv	ip	wat	nok
nav	pum	ved	iv	fof
ziz	tol	zan	duf	nev
ut	moj	jeb	tis	mas
al	jun	nek	fol	piv
hom	jij	kaf	dez	yup
sof	ij	jul	taj	hef
kem	hoz	zim	sak	un
lus	rej	yoj	ral	zis
yab	op	pij	sel	tun

▶ *Put your finger under the first word. Ready, begin.*

Timing	1 minute. Start your stopwatch after telling the student to begin. Place a bracket (**]**) and say **Stop** after 1 minute.
Wait	If the student responds sound-by-sound, mixes sounds and words, or sounds out and recodes, allow 3 seconds, then provide the correct letter sound.
	If the student responds with whole words, allow 3 seconds, then provide the correct word.
Discontinue	If the student has no correct letter sounds in the first line, say **Stop** and record a score of 0.
Reminders	If the student does not read from left to right, say **Go this way**. (Sweep your finger across the row.) (Allowed one time.)
	If the student says letter names, say **Say the sounds, not the letter names**. (Allowed one time.)
	If the student reads the word first, then says the letter sounds, say **Just read the word**. (Allowed one time.)
	If the student says all of the letter sounds correctly in the first row, but does not make any attempt to blend or recode, say **Try to read the words as whole words**.
	If the student stops (and it's not a hesitation on a specific item), say **Keep going**. (Repeat as often as needed.)
	If the student loses his/her place, point. (Repeat as often as needed.)

NWF

sog   mip

11 DIBELS® Nonsense Word Fluency
Progress Monitoring 11

Directions: Make sure you have reviewed the scoring rules in the *DIBELS Next Assessment Manual* and have them available. Say these specific directions to the student:

▶ *We are going to read some make-believe words. Listen. This word is "sog."* (Run your finger under the word as you say it.) *The sounds are /s/ /o/ /g/* (point to each letter). *Your turn. Read this make-believe word* (point to the word "mip"). *If you can't read the whole word, tell me any sounds you know.*

Correct Whole Word Read mip	**Very good reading the word "mip."**	(Begin testing.)

Correct Letter Sounds Any other response with all the correct letter sounds	**Very good. /m/ /i/ /p/** (point to each letter) **or "mip"** (run your finger under the word as you say it).	(Begin testing.)

Incorrect response No response within 3 <u>seconds</u>, or response includes any errors	**Listen. /m/ /i/ /p/ or "mip."** (Run your finger under the letters as you say the sounds.) **Your turn. Read this make-believe word.** (Point to the word "mip.") **If you can't read the whole word, tell me any sounds you know.**	Correct response	**Very good.**	(Begin testing.)
		Incorrect response	**Okay.**	(Begin testing.)

▶ **Begin testing.** *I would like you to read more make-believe words. Do your best reading. If you can't read the whole word, tell me any sounds you know.* Go to the next page.

▶ pip	duv	ak	wot	lep
fuz	mek	yig	aj	nof
yuv	kot	yep	sim	laj
ec	nov	yag	tup	dib
uk	yek	hob	bik	sav
dof	zaz	del	hiz	jub
bod	av	zed	kiz	dul
fem	foz	yal	lis	ul
bem	pav	yiv	num	vom
yis	ap	tez	buf	pos

11 DIBELS® Nonsense Word Fluency
Progress Monitoring 11 continued

▶ *Put your finger under the first word. Ready, begin.*

Timing	1 minute. Start your stopwatch after telling the student to begin. Place a bracket (**]**) and say ***Stop*** after 1 minute.
Wait	If the student responds sound-by-sound, mixes sounds and words, or sounds out and recodes, allow 3 seconds, then provide the correct letter sound. If the student responds with whole words, allow 3 seconds, then provide the correct word.
Discontinue	If the student has no correct letter sounds in the first line, say ***Stop*** and record a score of 0.
Reminders	If the student does not read from left to right, say ***Go this way***. (Sweep your finger across the row.) (Allowed one time.) If the student says letter names, say ***Say the sounds, not the letter names***. (Allowed one time.) If the student reads the word first, then says the letter sounds, say ***Just read the word***. (Allowed one time.) If the student says all of the letter sounds correctly in the first row, but does not make any attempt to blend or recode, say ***Try to read the words as whole words***. If the student stops (and it's not a hesitation on a specific item), say ***Keep going***. (Repeat as often as needed.) If the student loses his/her place, point. (Repeat as often as needed.)

NWF

sog   mip

12 DIBELS® Nonsense Word Fluency
Progress Monitoring 12

Directions: Make sure you have reviewed the scoring rules in the *DIBELS Next Assessment Manual* and have them available. Say these specific directions to the student:

▶ *We are going to read some make-believe words. Listen. This word is "sog."* (Run your finger under the word as you say it.) *The sounds are /s/ /o/ /g/* (point to each letter). *Your turn. Read this make-believe word* (point to the word "mip"). *If you can't read the whole word, tell me any sounds you know.*

Correct Whole Word Read mip	***Very good reading the word "mip."***	(Begin testing.)			
Correct Letter Sounds Any other response with all the correct letter sounds	***Very good. /m/ /i/ /p/*** (point to each letter) ***or "mip"*** (run your finger under the word as you say it).	(Begin testing.)			
Incorrect response No response within 3 <u>seconds</u>, or response includes any errors	***Listen. /m/ /i/ /p/ or "mip."*** (Run your finger under the letters as you say the sounds.) ***Your turn. Read this make-believe word.*** (Point to the word "mip.") ***If you can't read the whole word, tell me any sounds you know.***		*Correct response*	***Very good.***	(Begin testing.)
			Incorrect response	***Okay.***	(Begin testing.)

▶ Begin testing. *I would like you to read more make-believe words. Do your best reading. If you can't read the whole word, tell me any sounds you know.* Go to the next page.

▶ nid	tev	ab	wug	lon
boz	bak	zus	iv	nes
zuz	lif	yob	nec	kaj
ek	bov	yaf	dup	mib
od	jef	mif	fas	kuj
bab	yov	bub	fiz	vec
sed	ov	wuf	daj	rit
dak	loj	wum	kic	el
fac	lev	juj	hig	yon
jep	oc	lij	dal	lul

12 DIBELS® Nonsense Word Fluency
Progress Monitoring 12 continued

▶ *Put your finger under the first word. Ready, begin.*

Timing	1 minute. Start your stopwatch after telling the student to begin. Place a bracket (**]**) and say **Stop** after 1 minute.
Wait	If the student responds sound-by-sound, mixes sounds and words, or sounds out and recodes, allow 3 seconds, then provide the correct letter sound.
	If the student responds with whole words, allow 3 seconds, then provide the correct word.
Discontinue	If the student has no correct letter sounds in the first line, say **Stop** and record a score of 0.
Reminders	If the student does not read from left to right, say **Go this way**. (Sweep your finger across the row.) (Allowed one time.)
	If the student says letter names, say **Say the sounds, not the letter names**. (Allowed one time.)
	If the student reads the word first, then says the letter sounds, say **Just read the word**. (Allowed one time.)
	If the student says all of the letter sounds correctly in the first row, but does not make any attempt to blend or recode, say **Try to read the words as whole words**.
	If the student stops (and it's not a hesitation on a specific item), say **Keep going**. (Repeat as often as needed.)
	If the student loses his/her place, point. (Repeat as often as needed.)

sog   mip

13 DIBELS® Nonsense Word Fluency
Progress Monitoring 13

Directions: Make sure you have reviewed the scoring rules in the *DIBELS Next Assessment Manual* and have them available. Say these specific directions to the student:

▶ *We are going to read some make-believe words. Listen. This word is "sog."* (Run your finger under the word as you say it.) *The sounds are /s/ /o/ /g/* (point to each letter). *Your turn. Read this make-believe word* (point to the word "mip"). *If you can't read the whole word, tell me any sounds you know.*

Correct Whole Word Read mip	*Very good reading the word "mip."*	(Begin testing.)
Correct Letter Sounds Any other response with all the correct letter sounds	*Very good. /m/ /i/ /p/* (point to each letter) *or "mip"* (run your finger under the word as you say it).	(Begin testing.)

Incorrect response No response within 3 <u>seconds</u>, or response includes any errors	*Listen. /m/ /i/ /p/ or "mip."* (Run your finger under the letters as you say the sounds.) *Your turn. Read this make-believe word.* (Point to the word "mip.") *If you can't read the whole word, tell me any sounds you know.*	*Correct response*	*Very good.*	(Begin testing.)
		Incorrect response	*Okay.*	(Begin testing.)

▶ Begin testing. *I would like you to read more make-believe words. Do your best reading. If you can't read the whole word, tell me any sounds you know.* Go to the next page.

NWF

► nug	bej	ol	zam	sig
kiv	som	ven	uz	kad
voz	fet	jud	mal	riv
im	sev	zop	tud	raf
ud	jel	pic	nac	boj
fil	woz	pas	suj	zeg
pol	av	vip	buv	sef
rec	biv	yom	fud	ac
kak	dov	zej	nul	yik
vek	af	nij	sot	mul

13 DIBELS® Nonsense Word Fluency
Progress Monitoring 13 continued

▶ *Put your finger under the first word. Ready, begin.*

Timing	1 minute. Start your stopwatch after telling the student to begin. Place a bracket (**]**) and say **Stop** after 1 minute.
Wait	If the student responds sound-by-sound, mixes sounds and words, or sounds out and recodes, allow 3 seconds, then provide the correct letter sound. If the student responds with whole words, allow 3 seconds, then provide the correct word.
Discontinue	If the student has no correct letter sounds in the first line, say **Stop** and record a score of 0.
Reminders	If the student does not read from left to right, say **Go this way**. (Sweep your finger across the row.) (Allowed one time.) If the student says letter names, say **Say the sounds, not the letter names**. (Allowed one time.) If the student reads the word first, then says the letter sounds, say **Just read the word**. (Allowed one time.) If the student says all of the letter sounds correctly in the first row, but does not make any attempt to blend or recode, say **Try to read the words as whole words**. If the student stops (and it's not a hesitation on a specific item), say **Keep going**. (Repeat as often as needed.) If the student loses his/her place, point. (Repeat as often as needed.)

NWF

sog   mip

14 DIBELS® Nonsense Word Fluency
Progress Monitoring 14

Directions: Make sure you have reviewed the scoring rules in the *DIBELS Next Assessment Manual* and have them available. Say these specific directions to the student:

▶ *We are going to read some make-believe words. Listen. This word is "sog."* (Run your finger under the word as you say it.) *The sounds are /s/ /o/ /g/* (point to each letter). *Your turn. Read this make-believe word* (point to the word "mip"). *If you can't read the whole word, tell me any sounds you know.*

Correct Whole Word Read mip	**Very good reading the word "mip."**	(Begin testing.)

Correct Letter Sounds Any other response with all the correct letter sounds	**Very good. /m/ /i/ /p/** (point to each letter) **or "mip"** (run your finger under the word as you say it).	(Begin testing.)

Incorrect response No response within 3 <u>seconds</u>, or response includes any errors	**Listen. /m/ /i/ /p/ or "mip."** (Run your finger under the letters as you say the sounds.) **Your turn. Read this make-believe word.** (Point to the word "mip.") **If you can't read the whole word, tell me any sounds you know.**	Correct response	**Very good.**	(Begin testing.)
		Incorrect response	**Okay.**	(Begin testing.)

▶ **Begin testing.** *I would like you to read more make-believe words. Do your best reading. If you can't read the whole word, tell me any sounds you know.* **Go to the next page.**

▶ mab	soz	uc	wec	ric
suz	nic	veb	aj	moc
jiv	sul	wep	poc	tav
ob	mav	zud	leb	bif
eg	jup	dob	lic	dav
bip	wev	nal	foj	juk
pob	uv	yad	biz	tef
lok	kav	yul	pem	ik
tik	hov	wez	hud	wak
wek	um	fav	fos	ril

14 DIBELS® Nonsense Word Fluency
Progress Monitoring 14 continued

▶ *Put your finger under the first word. Ready, begin.*

Timing	1 minute. Start your stopwatch after telling the student to begin. Place a bracket ( ]) and say **Stop** after 1 minute.
Wait	If the student responds sound-by-sound, mixes sounds and words, or sounds out and recodes, allow 3 seconds, then provide the correct letter sound. If the student responds with whole words, allow 3 seconds, then provide the correct word.
Discontinue	If the student has no correct letter sounds in the first line, say **Stop** and record a score of 0.
Reminders	If the student does not read from left to right, say **Go this way**. (Sweep your finger across the row.) (Allowed one time.) If the student says letter names, say **Say the sounds, not the letter names**. (Allowed one time.) If the student reads the word first, then says the letter sounds, say **Just read the word**. (Allowed one time.) If the student says all of the letter sounds correctly in the first row, but does not make any attempt to blend or recode, say **Try to read the words as whole words**. If the student stops (and it's not a hesitation on a specific item), say **Keep going**. (Repeat as often as needed.) If the student loses his/her place, point. (Repeat as often as needed.)

NWF

sog   mip

15 DIBELS® Nonsense Word Fluency
Progress Monitoring 15

Directions: Make sure you have reviewed the scoring rules in the *DIBELS Next Assessment Manual* and have them available. Say these specific directions to the student:

▶ *We are going to read some make-believe words. Listen. This word is "sog."* (Run your finger under the word as you say it.) *The sounds are /s/ /o/ /g/* (point to each letter). *Your turn. Read this make-believe word* (point to the word "mip"). *If you can't read the whole word, tell me any sounds you know.*

Correct Whole Word Read mip	**Very good reading the word "mip."**	(Begin testing.)
Correct Letter Sounds Any other response with all the correct letter sounds	**Very good. /m/ /i/ /p/** (point to each letter) **or "mip"** (run your finger under the word as you say it).	(Begin testing.)

Incorrect response No response within 3 <u>seconds</u>, or response includes any errors	**Listen. /m/ /i/ /p/ or "mip."** (Run your finger under the letters as you say the sounds.) **Your turn. Read this make-believe word.** (Point to the word "mip.") **If you can't read the whole word, tell me any sounds you know.**	*Correct response*	**Very good.**	(Begin testing.)
		Incorrect response	**Okay.**	(Begin testing.)

▶ **Begin testing.** *I would like you to read more make-believe words. Do your best reading. If you can't read the whole word, tell me any sounds you know.* **Go to the next page.**

▶ tok	tiz	ep	vaf	dut
hej	sim	zuc	az	kos
vev	kan	wuk	fon	dij
ig	paj	jok	fel	kup
es	wil	mag	tob	kuz
pab	yev	sos	huj	zif
lat	ij	wef	fov	buk
pel	siv	zaf	nos	uf
hod	buj	yiz	ren	wan
wub	og	lav	bip	bek

▶ *Put your finger under the first word. Ready, begin.*

Timing	1 minute. Start your stopwatch after telling the student to begin. Place a bracket (**]**) and say **Stop** after 1 minute.
Wait	If the student responds sound-by-sound, mixes sounds and words, or sounds out and recodes, allow 3 seconds, then provide the correct letter sound.
	If the student responds with whole words, allow 3 seconds, then provide the correct word.
Discontinue	If the student has no correct letter sounds in the first line, say **Stop** and record a score of 0.
Reminders	If the student does not read from left to right, say **Go this way**. (Sweep your finger across the row.) (Allowed one time.)
	If the student says letter names, say **Say the sounds, not the letter names**. (Allowed one time.)
	If the student reads the word first, then says the letter sounds, say **Just read the word**. (Allowed one time.)
	If the student says all of the letter sounds correctly in the first row, but does not make any attempt to blend or recode, say **Try to read the words as whole words**.
	If the student stops (and it's not a hesitation on a specific item), say **Keep going**. (Repeat as often as needed.)
	If the student loses his/her place, point. (Repeat as often as needed.)

NWF

sog   mip

Directions: Make sure you have reviewed the scoring rules in the *DIBELS Next Assessment Manual* and have them available. Say these specific directions to the student:

▶ *We are going to read some make-believe words. Listen. This word is "sog."* (Run your finger under the word as you say it.) *The sounds are /s/ /o/ /g/* (point to each letter). *Your turn. Read this make-believe word* (point to the word "mip"). *If you can't read the whole word, tell me any sounds you know.*

Correct Whole Word Read mip	***Very good reading the word "mip."***	(Begin testing.)

Correct Letter Sounds Any other response with all the correct letter sounds	***Very good.*** */m/ /i/ /p/* (point to each letter) ***or "mip"*** (run your finger under the word as you say it).	(Begin testing.)

Incorrect response No response within 3 <u>seconds</u>, or response includes any errors	***Listen.*** */m/ /i/ /p/ **or "mip."*** (Run your finger under the letters as you say the sounds.) ***Your turn. Read this make-believe word.*** (Point to the word "mip.") ***If you can't read the whole word, tell me any sounds you know.***	*Correct response*	***Very good.***	(Begin testing.)
		Incorrect response	***Okay.***	(Begin testing.)

▶ **Begin testing.** *I would like you to read more make-believe words. Do your best reading. If you can't read the whole word, tell me any sounds you know.* **Go to the next page.**

▶ tik	tev	ot	wak	rul
poj	tig	yad	uj	feb
wuz	hoc	yil	taf	dev
eb	sij	wol	nan	kud
em	vup	fap	fid	moz
dit	joz	dem	taj	wup
tuk	oj	jed	mij	nak
mok	kev	vab	luk	id
fif	kez	wuv	nom	yas
jod	ug	hiv	kef	bap

16 DIBELS® Nonsense Word Fluency
Progress Monitoring 16 continued

▶ *Put your finger under the first word. Ready, begin.*

Timing	1 minute. Start your stopwatch after telling the student to begin. Place a bracket ( ]) and say **Stop** after 1 minute.
Wait	If the student responds sound-by-sound, mixes sounds and words, or sounds out and recodes, allow 3 seconds, then provide the correct letter sound. If the student responds with whole words, allow 3 seconds, then provide the correct word.
Discontinue	If the student has no correct letter sounds in the first line, say **Stop** and record a score of 0.
Reminders	If the student does not read from left to right, say **Go this way**. (Sweep your finger across the row.) (Allowed one time.) If the student says letter names, say **Say the sounds, not the letter names**. (Allowed one time.) If the student reads the word first, then says the letter sounds, say **Just read the word**. (Allowed one time.) If the student says all of the letter sounds correctly in the first row, but does not make any attempt to blend or recode, say **Try to read the words as whole words**. If the student stops (and it's not a hesitation on a specific item), say **Keep going**. (Repeat as often as needed.) If the student loses his/her place, point. (Repeat as often as needed.)

NWF

sog   mip

17 DIBELS® Nonsense Word Fluency
Progress Monitoring 17

Directions: Make sure you have reviewed the scoring rules in the *DIBELS Next Assessment Manual* and have them available. Say these specific directions to the student:

▶ *We are going to read some make-believe words. Listen. This word is "sog."* (Run your finger under the word as you say it.) *The sounds are /s/ /o/ /g/* (point to each letter). *Your turn. Read this make-believe word* (point to the word "mip"). *If you can't read the whole word, tell me any sounds you know.*

Correct Whole Word Read mip	*Very good reading the word "mip."*	(Begin testing.)
Correct Letter Sounds Any other response with all the correct letter sounds	*Very good. /m/ /i/ /p/* (point to each letter) *or "mip"* (run your finger under the word as you say it).	(Begin testing.)

Incorrect response No response within 3 <u>seconds</u>, or response includes any errors	*Listen. /m/ /i/ /p/ or "mip."* (Run your finger under the letters as you say the sounds.) *Your turn. Read this make-believe word.* (Point to the word "mip.") *If you can't read the whole word, tell me any sounds you know.*	*Correct response*	*Very good.*	(Begin testing.)
		Incorrect response	*Okay.*	(Begin testing.)

▶ *Begin testing. I would like you to read more make-believe words. Do your best reading. If you can't read the whole word, tell me any sounds you know.* Go to the next page.

▶ kap	tuz	ib	yel	rof
naj	bul	yog	iv	fef
yov	huk	vil	rac	lej
ag	liv	jos	tes	hup
os	zas	tis	nuk	rev
pog	vuv	dap	tez	wis
daf	ev	zul	foz	til
kop	saj	zif	hul	ef
rek	raj	zuj	ros	zim
yan	ub	koj	min	fek

▶ *Put your finger under the first word. Ready, begin.*

Timing	1 minute. Start your stopwatch after telling the student to begin. Place a bracket (**]**) and say *Stop* after 1 minute.
Wait	If the student responds sound-by-sound, mixes sounds and words, or sounds out and recodes, allow 3 seconds, then provide the correct letter sound. If the student responds with whole words, allow 3 seconds, then provide the correct word.
Discontinue	If the student has no correct letter sounds in the first line, say *Stop* and record a score of 0.
Reminders	If the student does not read from left to right, say *Go this way*. (Sweep your finger across the row.) (Allowed one time.) If the student says letter names, say *Say the sounds, not the letter names*. (Allowed one time.) If the student reads the word first, then says the letter sounds, say *Just read the word*. (Allowed one time.) If the student says all of the letter sounds correctly in the first row, but does not make any attempt to blend or recode, say *Try to read the words as whole words*. If the student stops (and it's not a hesitation on a specific item), say *Keep going*. (Repeat as often as needed.) If the student loses his/her place, point. (Repeat as often as needed.)

NWF

sog   mip

18 DIBELS® Nonsense Word Fluency
Progress Monitoring 18

Directions: Make sure you have reviewed the scoring rules in the *DIBELS Next Assessment Manual* and have them available. Say these specific directions to the student:

▶ *We are going to read some make-believe words. Listen. This word is "sog."* (Run your finger under the word as you say it.) *The sounds are /s/ /o/ /g/* (point to each letter). *Your turn. Read this make-believe word* (point to the word "mip"). *If you can't read the whole word, tell me any sounds you know.*

Correct Whole Word Read mip	***Very good reading the word "mip."***	(Begin testing.)
Correct Letter Sounds Any other response with all the correct letter sounds	***Very good.*** */m/ /i/ /p/* (point to each letter) ***or "mip"*** (run your finger under the word as you say it).	(Begin testing.)

Incorrect response No response within 3 <u>seconds</u>, or response includes any errors	***Listen.*** */m/ /i/ /p/ or "mip."* (Run your finger under the letters as you say the sounds.) ***Your turn. Read this make-believe word.*** (Point to the word "mip.") ***If you can't read the whole word, tell me any sounds you know.***	*Correct response*	***Very good.***	(Begin testing.)
		Incorrect response	***Okay.***	(Begin testing.)

▶ **Begin testing.** *I would like you to read more make-believe words. Do your best reading. If you can't read the whole word, tell me any sounds you know.* Go to the next page.

▶ kot	nez	uf	val	hib
nav	tel	wif	ov	hup
yuv	kik	zep	nan	lov
em	miz	wod	rud	kak
og	yus	mak	teg	tij
tid	voz	fum	bav	yed
luf	aj	yib	hoz	pef
nom	suv	jek	dat	ic
rab	suz	vez	bos	yil
wen	ob	bij	fud	sal

▶ *Put your finger under the first word. Ready, begin.*

Timing	1 minute. Start your stopwatch after telling the student to begin. Place a bracket (**]**) and say **Stop** after 1 minute.
Wait	If the student responds sound-by-sound, mixes sounds and words, or sounds out and recodes, allow 3 seconds, then provide the correct letter sound.
	If the student responds with whole words, allow 3 seconds, then provide the correct word.
Discontinue	If the student has no correct letter sounds in the first line, say **Stop** and record a score of 0.
Reminders	If the student does not read from left to right, say **Go this way**. (Sweep your finger across the row.) (Allowed one time.)
	If the student says letter names, say **Say the sounds, not the letter names**. (Allowed one time.)
	If the student reads the word first, then says the letter sounds, say **Just read the word**. (Allowed one time.)
	If the student says all of the letter sounds correctly in the first row, but does not make any attempt to blend or recode, say **Try to read the words as whole words**.
	If the student stops (and it's not a hesitation on a specific item), say **Keep going**. (Repeat as often as needed.)
	If the student loses his/her place, point. (Repeat as often as needed.)

NWF

sog   mip

19 DIBELS® Nonsense Word Fluency
Progress Monitoring 19

Directions: Make sure you have reviewed the scoring rules in the *DIBELS Next Assessment Manual* and have them available. Say these specific directions to the student:

▶ *We are going to read some make-believe words. Listen. This word is "sog."* (Run your finger under the word as you say it.) *The sounds are /s/ /o/ /g/* (point to each letter). *Your turn. Read this make-believe word* (point to the word "mip"). *If you can't read the whole word, tell me any sounds you know.*

Correct Whole Word Read mip	***Very good reading the word "mip."***	(Begin testing.)
Correct Letter Sounds Any other response with all the correct letter sounds	***Very good. /m/ /i/ /p/*** (point to each letter) ***or "mip"*** (run your finger under the word as you say it).	(Begin testing.)

Incorrect response No response within 3 <u>seconds</u>, or response includes any errors	***Listen. /m/ /i/ /p/ or "mip."*** (Run your finger under the letters as you say the sounds.) ***Your turn. Read this make-believe word.*** (Point to the word "mip.") ***If you can't read the whole word, tell me any sounds you know.***	Correct response	***Very good.***	(Begin testing.)
		Incorrect response	***Okay.***	(Begin testing.)

▶ Begin testing. *I would like you to read more make-believe words. Do your best reading. If you can't read the whole word, tell me any sounds you know.* Go to the next page.

► kup	tej	ab	woc	fis
huv	non	zed	ij	sak
zav	reb	yol	pik	luj
ac	pez	zuf	bik	mog
ec	wuf	nog	dak	siz
rep	yuz	fol	rav	jik
bef	oj	zil	fuz	faf
mos	fez	vis	pag	um
tak	buv	woj	hin	vec
vep	od	fuj	lil	laf

DIBELS® Nonsense Word Fluency
Progress Monitoring 19 continued

▶ *Put your finger under the first word. Ready, begin.*

Timing	1 minute. Start your stopwatch after telling the student to begin. Place a bracket ( ]) and say *Stop* after 1 minute.
Wait	If the student responds sound-by-sound, mixes sounds and words, or sounds out and recodes, allow 3 seconds, then provide the correct letter sound.
	If the student responds with whole words, allow 3 seconds, then provide the correct word.
Discontinue	If to student has no correct letter sounds in the first line, say *Stop* and record a score of 0.
Reminders	If the student does not read from left to right, say *Go this way*. (Sweep your finger across the row.) (Allowed one time.)
	If the student says letter names, say *Say the sounds, not the letter names*. (Allowed one time.)
	If the student reads the word first, then says the letter sounds, say *Just read the word*. (Allowed one time.)
	If the student says all of the letter sounds correctly in the first row, but does not make any attempt to blend or recode, say *Try to read the words as whole words*.
	If the student stops (and it's not a hesitation on a specific item), say *Keep going*. (Repeat as often as needed.)
	If the student loses his/her place, point. (Repeat as often as needed.)

NWF

sog   mip

20 DIBELS® Nonsense Word Fluency
Progress Monitoring 20

Directions: Make sure you have reviewed the scoring rules in the *DIBELS Next Assessment Manual* and have them available. Say these specific directions to the student:

▶ *We are going to read some make-believe words. Listen. This word is "sog."* (Run your finger under the word as you say it.) *The sounds are /s/ /o/ /g/* (point to each letter). *Your turn. Read this make-believe word* (point to the word "mip"). *If you can't read the whole word, tell me any sounds you know.*

Correct Whole Word Read mip	**Very good reading the word "mip."**	(Begin testing.)
Correct Letter Sounds Any other response with all the correct letter sounds	**Very good. /m/ /i/ /p/** (point to each letter) **or "mip"** (run your finger under the word as you say it).	(Begin testing.)

Incorrect response No response within 3 <u>seconds</u>, or response includes any errors	**Listen. /m/ /i/ /p/ or "mip."** (Run your finger under the letters as you say the sounds.) **Your turn. Read this make-believe word.** (Point to the word "mip.") **If you can't read the whole word, tell me any sounds you know.**	*Correct response*	**Very good.**	(Begin testing.)
		Incorrect response	**Okay.**	(Begin testing.)

▶ Begin testing. *I would like you to read more make-believe words. Do your best reading. If you can't read the whole word, tell me any sounds you know.* Go to the next page.

► kek	fiv	os	zul	hal
luv	ras	jof	iv	peb
yiz	lus	yel	kam	toz
ub	sez	zod	fas	hil
ap	zup	heg	bif	moj
nic	yav	lud	nej	zog
nof	uv	zak	sej	bil
pim	dej	jun	lan	op
bas	tuv	wej	tog	wic
jem	ug	tiv	rog	kal

▶ *Put your finger under the first word. Ready, begin.*

Timing	1 minute. Start your stopwatch after telling the student to begin. Place a bracket ( ]) and say *Stop* after 1 minute.
Wait	If the student responds sound-by-sound, mixes sounds and words, or sounds out and recodes, allow 3 seconds, then provide the correct letter sound. If the student responds with whole words, allow 3 seconds, then provide the correct word.
Discontinue	If the student has no correct letter sounds in the first line, say *Stop* and record a score of 0.
Reminders	If the student does not read from left to right, say *Go this way*. (Sweep your finger across the row.) (Allowed one time.) If the student says letter names, say *Say the sounds, not the letter names*. (Allowed one time.) If the student reads the word first, then says the letter sounds, say *Just read the word*. (Allowed one time.) If the student says all of the letter sounds correctly in the first row, but does not make any attempt to blend or recode, say *Try to read the words as whole words*. If the student stops (and it's not a hesitation on a specific item), say *Keep going*. (Repeat as often as needed.) If the student loses his/her place, point. (Repeat as often as needed.)

NWF